Say goodbay to routine ...

Copyright © 2021 by J.B Devoy

All rights reserved. This book or any portion thereof
may not be reproduced or used in any manner
whatsoever without the express written permission
of the publisher except for the use of brief
quotations in a book review.
Published by: J.B Devoy

Game rules

FOR COUPLE

Take turns and choose between Truth or Dare.
If you don't answer the truth questions or complete you dare, your partner can choose your punishment.

Game rules

FOR PARTY WITH FRIENDS

Make everyone sit in a circle.
Position a bottle in the center
in such a way that it can rotate easily.
Turn the bottle giving it a gentle push.
A truth or dare question needs
to be asked to the person at whom the
bottle stops rotating.
Each player can ask a question
by taking turns.
The question has to begin
with asking 'truth or dare'.
If the player selects truth, then ask a
question which needs to be answered
with utmost honesty.
If a player selects dare, then assign a
command or a daring act
to be performed.

The last three digits of your mobile number will tell you what you need the most

1 Sleep	**2** Love	**3** Sex
4 Rest	**5** Kiss	**6** Money
7 Thai massage	**8** Alcohol	**9** Oral sex
*****	**0** Hug	**#**

TRUTH

How many people
have you been
with sexually?

or

Tell the person you find
most attractive right now
what exactly you would
like to do to him/her.

DARE

TRUTH

How many people
have you been
with at one time?

or

Lick my toes after
I have dipped them
in your ass.

DARE

TRUTH

Would you have
a threesome
with your ex
and her/him
new partner?

or

Pick a random person
on your phone
and tell them
you would like
to give them oral sex.

DARE

TRUTH

What was your
last sex dream like?

or

Do exactly whatever
you dreamed about,
no matter how kinky it was.

DARE

TRUTH

Have you ever sucked the cock of more than one man at a time?

or

Lick my ass.

DARE

TRUTH

Would you fuck someone
you just met
in a club bathroom?

or

Send a suggestive
text message
to someone in your phone.

DARE

Do you have a fetish
that you haven't
told anyone,
one that you
wouldn't want
others to know about?

or

Lick my balls while
you masturbate.

TRUTH

Have you ever fucked
in front of several people?

or

Get naked and record
yourself with your phone
while masturbating,
and say my name
directly to the camera.

DARE

TRUTH

Would you let someone
who hasn't had a shower
in days fuck you?

or

Put your finger
in your pussy,
and then lick your fingers.

DARE

TRUTH

Have you had sexual
fantasies with women
you consider friends?

or

Ask one of your friends
to come over here
and eat your pussy.

DARE

TRUTH

Have you ever fucked someone you hated?

or

Strip me using only your mouth.

DARE

Has anyone ever thrown up on you while sucking your dick?

Run your tongue through my armpit.

TRUTH

Would you ever
date someone
you didn't like very much?

 or

Invite the first person
who appears to you
as your contact on Whatsap
to go out.

DARE

TRUTH

Who did you think
of last time
you masturbated?

or

Masturbate and masturbate
at the same time
without stopping.
Without changing hands.

DARE

TRUTH

Who would you be
unfaithful to?

 **or**

Lick my balls while
masturbating, and look me
straight in the eye.

DARE

TRUTH

Have you ever been
with a professor
to pass subjects in college?

or

Get me excited just
by telling me the things
you would like to do to me.

DARE

TRUTH

Have you ever seen pornography that you're a little embarrassed to admit to right now?

or

Pick a person at random and tell them your most embarrassing sexual memory.

DARE

TRUTH

Would you have sex
with another person
and allow me to watch?

or

Swallow my entire run
without dropping anything.

DARE

TRUTH

Have you ever masturbated thinking about someone inappropriate?

or

Tell me everything you want to do to me while you undress me.

DARE

TRUTH

Do you like it when
I talk dirty to you
when we fuck?

or

Let's tape ourselves
having sex.

DARE

TRUTH

Have you ever faked
an exaggerated orgasm?

 **or**

Propose the most indecent
and dirty thing you can
think of to a friend
without telling them
later that it was a challenge.

DARE

TRUTH

Would you sleep with me
all night without
ever having sex?

or

I'll get naked for 20 minutes,
and you can't touch me.
 I'll walk around the room,
you can only watch.

DARE

TRUTH

Have you ever
had group sex?

or

Send a picture of your dick
to someone at random.

DARE

TRUTH

Have you been with someone at work?

or

Take a picture with my dick in your mouth.

DARE

Have you ever gotten aroused in public place thinking about someone you like?

or

Put on this costume and meow.

TRUTH

Who have you liked sex
with the most?

or

Encourage phone sex
with one of your contacts.

DARE

TRUTH

Have you ever fucked while watching porn and imitated what's going on in the movie?

or

Describe the best sex of your life in three words.

DARE

TRUTH

Have you lied to get sex?

or

Put my dick between your tits, and make me come.

DARE

TRUTH

Have you ever shared a bed with someone else while you were with me?

or

Rate me 1 to 10 on sex..

DARE

TRUTH

Do you like it to be very loud while we fuck?

or

Put a toe in your mouth, and look at me erotically while you do it.

DARE

TRUTH

Do you like role-playing?

or

Let's rub each other completely naked, and then you have to go half an hour without fucking.

DARE

TRUTH

Anything different
you want to do in sex?

 **or**

Rub my leg for 15 minutes .

DARE

TRUTH

Have you ever danced
sensually for someone?

or

Do a lap dance
for five minutes.

DARE

TRUTH

Have you ever kissed
more than one person
in one night?

or

Choose the most unusual
part of your body where
you want your tongue to go.

DARE

TRUTH

What is the most
inappropriate place
you have ever had sex?

or

Give me a massage for 10
minutes.

DARE

TRUTH

Have you ever had sex
in your parents' bed?

 **or**

Excite me by using only
one hand, touching any part
of my body.

DARE

Have you ever done
Gangbang?

or

Let's make a video call
while we're fucking.

TRUTH

Have you done double
penetration?

Rub your dick against
my ass without
penetrating me.

DARE

TRUTH

Have you made someone
desire you without
you desiring that person?

or

Spread peanut butter
on my crotch, and remove it
all using your tongue.

DARE

TRUTH

Have you ever made
pet play?

or

Go out of the house naked,
stand right in front
of the house
for 30 seconds.

DARE

Do you like it slow or fast?

Put a mint in your mouth
and give me oral sex.

TRUTH

What fantasy would you like to fulfill that you haven't talked about?

or

Kiss me without using your hands.You can't touch me, just touch my lips with yours.

DARE

TRUTH

Would you like to seduce
someone else?

 or

Try singing while
you are giving me
oral sex.

DARE

TRUTH

What wouldn't you like to do
while we are fucking?

or

Whisper to me what you
don't want me to do to you
in the most sensual
way possible.

DARE

TRUTH

Do you like sex standing up
or lying down better?

or

Wear sexy lingerie while
we play,change your clothes
slowly while looking into
my eyes.

DARE

What would you think
of me if you found
me masturbating?

Do a foot job on me.

TRUTH

What secrets have you kept
from me?

or

Suck my wet fingers
after pulling them
out of your pussy.

DARE

TRUTH

What would you think
if someone you like
confessed to being bisexual?

 **or**

Take a picture of your pussy
with your legs wide open
and send it to my phone.

DARE

TRUTH

Have you ever discarded someone simply because you didn't like a part of their body?

 **or**

Let's take a bath together and pee on me.

DARE

TRUTH

Would you do oral sex
on someone who
has their period?

or

Lick my ass without
running my tongue
through my pussy.

DARE

TRUTH

What was the most unpleasant thing that happened to you during sex?

 **or**

Rubbing and fondling each other's clothes without getting naked for a long period of time.

DARE

TRUTH

Have you had sex for a whole
month without stopping
for a single day?

or

Just pull out your dick,
and let's fuck with
our clothes on.

DARE

TRUTH

Do you like to have sex
sober or drunk?

or

Call your ex and tell her/him
that you left him because
you no longer found
him attractive.

DARE

TRUTH

Have you ever had sex
with a neighbor ?

Have a conversation
via Whatsapp with someone
about your sexual
fantasies for five minutes.

DARE

TRUTH

What's the strangest place someone has ever asked you to have sex?

 or

Give me a stop massage .

DARE

TRUTH

Have you ever been caught
having sex?

or

Put your index finger
in your own butt,
and then put it
in your mouth.

DARE

TRUTH

Have you lied about
the number of sexual
partners you've had?

or

I will give you oral sex while
inserting my finger in your ass.
You can't say anything.

DARE

TRUTH

Have you ever let yourself
be carried away
by someone's appearance?

or

Put on a maid's costume
for the rest of the game
with nothing underneath.

DARE

TRUTH

Do school uniforms
turn you on?

or

Bark while we have sex,
as loud as you can.

DARE

TRUTH

If you were invisible
would you spy on someone
in their room?
Who would you spy on?

Hold my cock in your throat
for several seconds
without gagging.

DARE

TRUTH

Have you ever had sex
with someone that you think
is unattractive?

or

Sink your head between
my legs while I push
your head further and further,
without coming to the surface
for 20 seconds.

DARE

TRUTH

What was the strangest
thing that turned you on,
and did you end
up masturbating?

or

Whatever I tell you right now,
we'll do it no matter
how crazy it sounds,
and then you yell at me
at the top of your lungs
as if it were your idea.

DARE

TRUTH

How do you like sex better
in or out of bed?

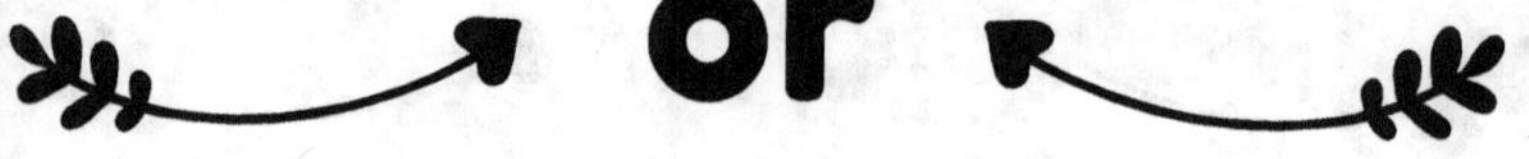

or

Stick your tongue
up your nose.

DARE

TRUTH

How do you like sex best,
outside or in the room?

 or

Take my hand, and teach me
how to masturbate
exactly how you want.

DARE

TRUTH

Have your parents ever caught you masturbating?

or

Take a shot of tequila from between my tits.

DARE

Have you ever taken
someone's virginity?

 or

Sit on my face.

TRUTH

Have you ever been attracted to a friend's partner?

 or

Look out the window naked and scream that you need sex.

DARE

TRUTH

Do you like to be humiliated
during sex?

or

Choose any lingerie you like
and dress me exactly
the way you want.

DARE

TRUTH

If you could change
one thing about the person
you are with,
what would it be?

or

Caress me without using
your hands, only with your
face, or any part of your body.

DARE

TRUTH

Do you like dirty sex a lot?

 or

I will go to pee,
and then suck, kiss my pussy
for several minutes.

DARE

Have you ever had sex
at the beach, or in the pool?

or

I will pass an ice cube
up your ass.

TRUTH

Have you ever regretted having sex with someone?

or

Do naked squats on my dick.

DARE

Would you do a three-way kiss?

Masturbate in front of the mirror making many faces of pleasure.

TRUTH

Did your parents give
you the sex talk?
How did it go?

 **or**

Wear my lingerie
for 10 minutes.

DARE

At what age did you lose your virginity?

or

Give me very quick laps just on the clitoris.

TRUTH

Have you ever masturbated
thinking about someone
you consider unattractive?
And if you have,
why did you do it
if you consider that
person unattractive?

or

Tell me something in my ear
that makes my heart race,
something I can't refuse.

DARE

TRUTH

Have you ever been with someone much older than yourself just for the money?

or

Let me hit you lightly in the balls.

DARE

TRUTH

What kind of clothes do you
fantasize about with me?

 or

Act like a porn star while I'm
fucking you.

DARE

TRUTH

Would you have sex with someone who smells bad?

Wrap your hair around my dick and masturbate like that.

DARE

TRUTH

Have you ever been asked to take a bath before you fuck?

or

Put your dick between my toes.

DARE

TRUTH

Have you ever told someone that you have dreamt about fucking that person without being true?

 **or**

Spit on my chest and then lick everything without leaving anything behind.

DARE

TRUTH

What would you do
if someone lay on your bed
naked and told you
not to touch anything?

or

Buy a sex toy and send it
to a family member.

DARE

TRUTH

What wouldn't you let them
do to you in bed?

 or

Lick my nipples. Use only your
tongue, no sucking.

DARE

TRUTH

Have you ever been
too fast?

or

Kiss my neck while saying
erotic things in my ear,
make me wet.

DARE

TRUTH

Have you ever passed gas
while having sex?

Stick two fingers in my pussy,
and one in my ass.

DARE

TRUTH

Do you keep all the naked
pictures they send you?

or

Show me some.

DARE

TRUTH

Did you sneak out
in the middle of the night
to have sex?

Change your Whatsapp
profile picture to one
that shows you naked
for 20 seconds.

DARE

TRUTH

Have you ever cried
during sex?

or

Name the parts of my body
where you would like
to put your dick.

DARE

TRUTH

Have you ever fucked
a pregnant woman?

 **or**

Put your dick in my armpit;
fuck it as if it were my pussy.

DARE

TRUTH

Have you ever kissed
someone with bad breath?

or

I will cover my whole body
with chocolate, and try
to remove it all using
your tongue, without using
your hands.

DARE

TRUTH

Have you ever fucked
in college?

or

Let me gently fuck
your penis.

DARE

TRUTH

Have you ever imagined someone watching you fuck?

or

I will blindfold you and do whatever I want.

DARE

If someone offered
you money to fuck
in an environment with
questionable hygiene,
would you do it?

or

Stay tied up for a few
minutes.

TRUTH

Anything you like during sex
that you are ashamed
to admit?

 **or**

You can't make any noise
while I fuck you violently
for a few minutes.

DARE

TRUTH

Would you sleep with an old
woman or man?

or

I'll eat several things,
you kiss me and you'll
have to guess what
I've eaten.

DARE

Would you always like to use
dildos, or the cock is better?

Spread spicy on my nipples
and then put them
in your mouth.

TRUTH

What was the longest sexual relationship you have ever had and how long did it last?

 **or**

Invite some of your random contacts to have sex with us, don't tell them it's a challenge.

DARE

Would you like to have
a longer or thicker dick?

or

Pretend to be a bitch
walking on all fours.

DARE

TRUTH

If you had to choose between only oral sex or only penetrative sex for the rest of your life which one would you pick?

or

Close your eyes, scroll through your contact list and send a suggestive text message to someone in your phone.

DARE

TRUTH

Would you sleep
with someone on the first
date in the restaurant
bathroom?

 **or**

Recite me a very erotic poem
that you improvise
on the way.

DARE

www.ingramcontent.com/pod-product-compliance
Lightning Source LLC
Chambersburg PA
CBHW070815240726
48654CB00007B/354